THE LONDON UNDERGROUND

Andrew Emmerson

SHIRE PUBLICATIONS

Published in Great Britain in 2010 by Shire Publications
Ltd, Midland House, West Way, Botley, Oxford OX2 0PH,
United Kingdom.

44-02 23rd Street, Suite 219, Long Island City, NY 11101,
USA.

E-mail: shire@shirebooks.co.uk   www.shirebooks.co.uk

A CIP catalogue record for this book is available from the
British Library.

Shire Library no. 597   ISBN-13: 978 0 74780 790 2

Andrew Emmerson has asserted his right under the
Copyright, Designs and Patents Act, 1988, to be identified
as the author of this book.

Designed by Tony Truscott Designs, Sussex, UK
and typeset in Perpetua and Gill Sans.

Printed in China through Worldprint Ltd.

10 11 12 13 14   11 10 9 8 7 6 5 4 3 2

COVER IMAGE
An A. N. Wolstenholme drawing for the cover of an Ian
Allan ABC spotters' book.

TITLE PAGE IMAGE
Avoid delay and travel by the Underground, by unknown
artist, 1910.

CONTENTS PAGE IMAGE
Cross-section view of Baker Street station, drawn in 1860
before construction had begun.

ACKNOWLEDGEMENTS
Grateful thanks go to all those who provided assistance, in
particular the staff of the London Transport Museum and
the following individuals: Mike Ashton, Nick Catford, Neil
Johannessen, John Liffen, Roger Morgan, Tim Robinson,
Keith Ward, Hywel Williams and members of Subterranea
Britannica. Without their valuable contributions this book
would have been a far poorer affair.

Thanks are also due to the people and organisations who
allowed copyright photographs to be reproduced. These
are acknowledged as follows: Owen Dunn page 60,
London Transport Museum, cover, title page and pages 7
(bottom), 8 (top), 9, 10 (top), 11 (top), 12, 14 (bottom),
18, 20 (bottom), 21 (top), 22, 23, 26, 27 (top), 30, 31
(bottom), 33, 34 (top two), 38 (top), 39 (top), 43 (top
and bottom), 44, 46, 47, 49 (bottom), 50 (top), 52, 55,
56, 57 (top), 58 (bottom), and 63; Chris McKenna, pages
58 (top) and 59; Oxyman, pages 30 and 31; Panhard, page
54; Pmox, page 35; Dr Volkmar Rudolf, page 34; and
Chris J. Wood, page 57. The remainder of the illustrations
are from the author's own collection. A few of the
illustrations are taken from old documents and are not up
to today's reproduction standards.

Shire Publications is supporting the Woodland Trust, the UK's leading woodland conservation charity, by funding the dedication of trees.

CONTENTS

STEAM, SMUTS AND SULPHUR

IN 1860 work began to construct London's Metropolitan Railway. A pioneer in every sense, the railway gave its name to the metro systems that many major cities have today. But why London, and why underground rather than overhead, as in other cities around the world?

In the mid-nineteenth century London was the largest city in the world and traffic congestion in the streets was at least as bad as today. Public pressure for a faster alternative to horse-drawn buses and hansom cabs was intense. From the 1840s various schemes were proposed for overhead and underground railways but only one made it to reality – the private enterprise Metropolitan Railway, which opened in 1863. Constructing a railway on arches or pillars would have involved much demolition and opposition, leaving a route in tunnels and cuttings the only viable solution.

Fortunately there was no shortage of technical expertise in construction of this kind and only the scale of the enterprise was abnormal. Following the engineering practice of those days, the pioneer sub-surface lines used full-size trains (as on mainline railways) and were constructed about 16 feet below the surface in shallow cuttings and tunnels. These were built using the 'cut and cover' technique in which a cutting is dug and then roofed over. Occasionally problems did present themselves, however. When the Circle Line was constructed between Paddington and Bayswater in the late 1860s it was necessary to demolish two houses in an exclusive terrace called Leinster Gardens. To mitigate this blight, the gap in the houses was filled by 'dummy' buildings that are in fact mere façades 5 feet deep. The illusion is extremely convincing and numbers 23 and 24 Leinster Gardens are complete with railings, doors and ornamental plants (but no letterboxes).

In those days steam was the dominant source of power, so the use of steam locomotives was inevitable. Great efforts were made to ensure the engines would consume their own exhaust but this was largely unachievable, meaning that passengers (and staff) had to suffer clouds of steam as well as sooty smuts and sulphurous fumes from the smoke.

Opposite: This illustration from a children's book of 1883 conveys well the smoky atmosphere of Portland Road (now Great Portland Street) station in steam days. Note the numerous advertisements, gas globes for illumination and clouds of smoke. Hanging signs indicated where the first-class carriages stopped.

The first underground railways were constructed by the 'cut and cover' method, in which a wide trench was dug, lined with bricks and then arched over. A hoist lowered materials and brought spoil to the surface. The drawing was made at King's Cross in late 1861.

Travel in this smoky atmosphere made quite an impression on travellers, particularly foreigners such as the American writer Elizabeth Robins Pennell, who stated that every ticket bought represented a plunge into the unknown and sometimes an unpleasant one. She wrote:

On one of London's murky summer days I would go to much trouble and more expense to escape the plunge into the underground's hot vapour bath. In all weathers and seasons there are certain stations I would prefer to avoid. The foreigner, eager to know from the beginning the worst that can be, has only to make his first descent at Baker Street, Gower Street or Portland Road. Ten chances to one he will never have courage for a second. But it is only in these northern stations that one is choked and stifled beyond endurance. They were the earliest built, and they occur on that part of the line where ground is highest and therefore cuttings deepest. At the stations along the Thames and those to the east and west matters are vastly improved, and none but the over-fastidious will find them in ordinary London weather impossible.

Despite the underground railway's shortcomings, it was an immediate success and the original line from Paddington to Farringdon Street was soon extended, with branch lines running out into the suburbs. A second company, the District Railway, sprang up a year after the Metropolitan and the two companies extended their routes to create a continuous route that we know today as the Circle Line. The Metropolitan's route skirted the northern side of central London, while the District took a more southerly route, their lines meeting at South Kensington in the west and Tower Hill

THE UNDERGROUND RAILWAYS

Stoker. " Wery sorry to disturb yer at supper, ladies, but could yer oblige me with a scuttle o' coals for our engine, as we've run short of 'em this journey ? "

in the east. Fierce rivalry between the two companies resulted in extravagant advertising wars, with each company claiming to offer the shorter or faster route. This contention carried on after they shared operation of the Circle Line, which in those days was known as the Inner Circle to distinguish it

It did not take long for cartoonists to spot the humour in the new underground railway. This example from *Punch* magazine is both ridiculous and delightfully surreal.

The dummy houses at 23 and 24 Leinster Gardens, Bayswater, have fooled many a delivery boy.

At Ray Street, close to Farringdon station, the Circle Line tracks flooded more than once following heavy thunderstorms. In May 1915 the steam pump on the front of this locomotive is pumping away the water.

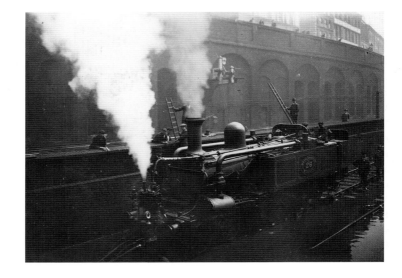

Rush hour, 1890s style. The title of this 1896 drawing of Mansion House station is 'Arrival of the City Men, 10 a.m.'. For City gentlemen, employment was clearly more leisurely in those days.

from the Middle and Outer Circles, which were operated over the Underground in part by other railway companies.

The focus now turned to extending the warring companies' lines into the suburbs, in order to generate greater revenue from longer journeys. Not all of these extensions were brand-new constructions: in many cases they reached their destinations by sharing the tracks of other existing railway companies. The District reached West Brompton in 1870 and Richmond via Hammersmith in 1869. Ealing ('the queen of the suburbs') was reached in 1879, and Fulham in 1880. District trains ran as far as Windsor in 1883 (withdrawn two years later), then to Hounslow via Acton in 1885, and finally to Wimbledon in 1889. During the same period the Metropolitan was setting its targets on the north-western suburbs and its so-called 'extension line' reached Harrow in 1880, Rickmansworth in 1887, Chesham in 1889 and Verney Junction (nearly 60 miles north of London) in 1894. By now the Metropolitan and District were proper suburban railways.

The co-operation with the existing 'big' railway companies did not end at track-sharing arrangements. In return for being granted 'running powers' over their lines, both the Metropolitan and the District allowed mainline trains to run over the Underground to enable their commuters to travel closer into central London or cross from one side of London to the other. Suburban trains from the west and north of London penetrated over the Circle Line as far as Moorgate and Mansion House, while for many years a through train service ran from Ealing in the west to Southend-on-Sea in the east. Freight trains of the main-line companies also used the Underground to reach their goods depots in the City of London. The Metropolitan had ambitions of itself becoming a main-line company, something that might easily have become reality. The company's far-sighted chairman, Sir Edward Watkin, held the same position on the Great Central and South Eastern Railways and sat on the board of the Northern Railway of France. His grand vision of linking these lines to create a through service from Manchester to Paris was frustrated only by the political and financial problems bound up with constructing a Channel Tunnel.

Underground train travel was for many people the wonder of the age, and naturally it featured in contemporary literature. The late 1880s onwards were the era of Sherlock Holmes, so unsurprisingly the Underground features in Conan Doyle's stories about the fictional detective. Holmes himself preferred the hansom cab but his other characters were not so fussy. His client in *The Adventure of the Beryl Coronet*, Alexander Holder, states: 'I came to Baker Street by the Underground.' In *The Red-Headed League*, Watson tells Holmes: 'We travelled by the Underground as far as Aldersgate.' Meanwhile, in *The Adventure of the Bruce-Partington Plans*, the dead body of Cadogan West is

Below ground, Mansion House station was a vast affair with several platforms for both Circle Line and longer-distance suburban routes now forgotten. Steam locomotives were also serviced here. At the centre of the lithograph is an early colour-light signal operated by gas.

9

discovered by a platelayer just outside Aldgate station, and the subsequent detail shows that Holmes knew plenty about the operation of the Metropolitan Railway. One of the rivals of Sherlock Holmes was the London detective created soon after 1900 by Baroness Orczy, and the Metropolitan Railway features in her story *The Mysterious Death on the Underground Railway*. A woman passenger is poisoned in

Without seeing this poster from 1919, few people would believe that District Line trains ran for many years as far as Southend-on-Sea.

Giant signs helped draw attention to newly built stations on the London Underground. This example served Monument station after it was opened in 1884.

Compartments like this (first-class of course) would have looked familiar to Sherlock Holmes. Remarkably these steam-era coaches remained in use until 1961 on the Metropolitan Line.

Electric trains replaced steam on the Metropolitan, District and Circle lines from 1903 onwards. The cavernous stations and their gas lamps remained unmodernised, however.

a first-class compartment and by a remarkable coincidence the death is discovered at Aldgate station.

Success came at a price, however. When the Underground opened in 1863 the only other public transport was slow horse buses, so passengers were prepared to tolerate the smoky atmosphere for a shorter journey time. By the turn of the new century there was fierce competition from electric trams, which passengers saw as clean and up-to-date. The smoke-ridden Metropolitan and District Railways both realised that electrification was inevitable if they were to stay in business and, following joint experiments in electric traction, they both began converting their lines to electric operation, the District in 1903 and the Metropolitan a year later. By 1907 all passenger trains over the Circle Line were electrically operated and steam had been banished apart from a few goods trains operating at night.

CENTRAL LONDON (TUBE) RAILWAY.

TAKING THE TICKET AT BANK STATION.

No worry about price
2ᵈ any distance

DISPOSING OF THE TICKET.

All tickets dropped into this box
No worry about losing them

SAFE & COMMODIOUS LIFTS.

TAKE
THE
TWO PENNY
TUBE

No Worry about accidents

AND
AVOID
ALL
ANXIETY

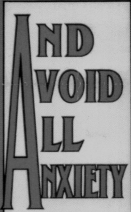

SHEPHERD'S BUSH. — HOLLAND PARK. — NOTTING HILL GATE. — QUEEN'S Rᵈ. — LANCASTER GATE. — MARBLE ARCH. — BOND Sᵀ. — OXFORD CIRCUS. — TOTTENHAM COURT Rᵈ. — BRITISH MUSEUM. — CHANCERY LANE. — POST OFFICE. — THE BANK.

CENTRAL LONDON RAILWAY.

ENTERING THE TRAIN.

Trains every few minutes
No worry about catching them

LEAVING THE STATION AT SHEPHERD'S BUSH.

The whole distance covered so quickly
that there's nothing to worry about.

PRINTED & PHOTO BY JOHNSON RIDDLE COLOURMAKERS LONDON S.E.

OXFORD CIRCUS STATION, LW.

GRANVILLE C. CUNINGHAM
GENERAL MANAGER

ARCS AND SPARKS

THE UNDERGROUND railways described in the previous chapter were all constructed just below the surface, more or less at basement level. Three decades after these first-generation lines began, a more radical kind of underground railway was launched – the deep-bore tube – deep, because it was built at much greater depths, and a bored tube, because it was constructed by digging or boring horizontally into the clay and lining the circular tunnel with iron segments that formed a tube. These true tube railways run at a deeper level (typically 60 feet below the surface), with each track running in a separate 12-foot-diameter tunnel that was bored horizontally using some kind of tunnelling shield. Because this entirely new construction technique took time to develop, and far greater expenditure, it is not surprising that the first proper tube railway did not open until 1890. In the spirit of the new era, the new trains were driven by electricity – steam was totally out of the question.

The first of these deep-level tubes ran from a City station at King William Street, near the Monument, out into the suburbs at Stockwell. Its original and highly logical name was the City and South London Subway; the word 'Subway' was changed to 'Railway' before opening but the original name caught the imagination of American observers so that tube railways in the United States were thenceforth always called 'subways'. The line opened in November 1890 and shortcomings soon began to appear. Very much pioneers, its constructors had made various decisions that seemed reasonable enough at the time but soon proved ill-advised. For instance, their logic indicated that passengers would have no interest in looking out at blank tunnel walls on their journey, so only small windows were provided just below roof level. Passengers were expected to find out where they were by listening for the name of the station, which was called out when the train stopped. This was little help for passengers who were deaf or unable to understand Cockney accents, and some inevitably missed their station. The platforms were rather narrow and poorly lit, while sharp curves and sudden steep gradients made the ride less than pleasant. Finally, the City terminus

Opposite:
The Central London Railway (today's Central Line) made the going easy by charging a flat fare of 2d for any journey. The mention of no worry about accidents in the lifts may have caused some passengers more anxiety than reassurance, however.

In contrast to the Metropolitan and District railways (which ran in shallow tunnels or cuttings), the tube railways ran in circular tubes at much deeper levels.

Few photographs survive of the original City and South London Railway's City terminus at King William Street. This picture was taken in 1899, a year before a replacement station was opened at Bank. Passengers travelled in so-called 'padded cell' coaches, hauled by a small four-wheeled electric locomotive.

was poorly located off the beaten track and passengers bound for London Bridge station or offices nearby had to cross the bridge on foot. All these defects were corrected but this took time.

Driving these first tubes through the London clay was done with the aid of a 'Greathead shield', a circular device rather like a giant apple corer. Inside this, men dug out the clay and shovelled it to the rear, where it was put into small trucks to be taken to the surface at a vertical service shaft. A subsequent improvement was the rotary excavator, which used rotating cutters driven by electricity. In both cases the shield was driven forward by hydraulic rams, with circular tunnel segments of iron (later concrete) placed into position to line the newly dug tunnel. Today more sophisticated tunnel-boring machines are used. These are self-driven, with a rotating cutting wheel at the front end of the shield. The excavated soil is either mixed with slurry and pumped out, or left for ejection by conveyor belt. Progress is rapid and requires only a few staff.

The colour and designs of tiling at the older tube stations were not chosen at random. A different colour scheme and pattern was applied to each station, enabling regular passengers to identify their station even if they could not see its name from the carriage window.

A question that puzzles many people is how the engineers working in the late nineteenth century ensured that their tunnels would meet within a fraction of an inch. For qualified civil engineers this was not a major problem: the line

of route was first surveyed above ground and accurate plans were drawn. At the vertical access shafts, points measured on the surface are transferred below ground using a pair of wires equipped with plumb weights. A sighting telescope or theodolite set up in the tunnel heading was then used to survey the plumb-lines below ground and then set the bearing and direction of the new tunnel. As the bore progressed, a series of plumb-lines and boning rods hung from the tunnel roof enabled the engineers to check the direction and level of the tunnel, making corrections as required. Fundamentally similar methods are used today, although laser sight-lines and reflective targets make the task simpler and faster.

The City and South London proved the concept of tube railways brilliantly and is still with us today as part of the Northern Line. Elizabeth Robins Pennell was an early supporter, even if some aspects were not to her taste. She wrote in 1896:

> The journey for the unaccustomed has an element of novelty. You are carried down to the platform and up again in an elevator. There is no division of classes, and the cars are built somewhat on the model of street cars; three are attached to each engine. I found the light – though it may have been a chance that one day – atrociously bad, the jolting dreadful, and the stations clean and dull compared to those on the ordinary underground. For, of course, there is no smoke, and the tiled walls are immaculately clean; as up and down lines have each a separate tube or tunnel, there is a platform but

This is the 'Greathead shield', which made the tunnelling of the early tube railways possible. Workmen at the front of the shield (where the man is standing) excavated clay so that the shield could be pushed forward. Iron tunnel segments (foreground) were then installed and bolted together.

to one side, and it is made as narrow and contracted as may be. The absence of smoke is an advantage in a way: the atmosphere may savor of the cellar, but there is no danger of being stifled and suffocated by foul air. The cleaner atmosphere of the electric [rail] road is not to be underestimated.

For many years the busier stations of the Northern Line were extremely cramped, as this painting of Bank station in the rush hour c.1910 shows. By then full-depth windows had been introduced but the carriages were still hauled by electric locomotives and had end entrances only, with gates operated manually by gatemen.

After this success new tube railways came thick and fast. The Waterloo and City (from Waterloo station to the Bank) opened in 1898; the Central London Railway (now Central Line) in 1900; the Great Northern & City Railway (now part of Network Rail) in 1904; and the Baker Street and Waterloo (soon renamed Bakerloo) in 1906, the same year that the Piccadilly Railway opened. The last new tube railway was the Hampstead Tube of 1907, which is now part of the Northern Line.

This rapid expansion did not come easily for the promoters, who faced heavy costs constructing and running their systems. For the money they required, several companies were forced to look to financiers, who some historians have likened to robber barons. Chief among these was Charles Tyson Yerkes, an American whose bribery, blackmail and crooked dealing had led him to prison. In the USA, Yerkes and his business partners succeeded

in gaining control of much of Chicago's streetcar and suburban railway operations; they then sought to repeat their success in London. In just five years Yerkes succeeded in gaining control of the District Railway and four tube lines, as well as securing the necessary finance to transform the steam-operated District into an all-electric line. Although he died in 1905, his fundraising involvement in London passenger transport continued to bear fruit, and his company, soon to be known as Underground Electric Railways

Passengers at Bank station (Central Line) in 1903. Before taking the lift down to platform level, travellers bought a 2d ticket (flat fare to any station) and then dropped it into a box (visible in the centre) under the gaze of a ticket inspector.

From opening day, trains on the new Piccadilly tube were bright and roomy, as this publicity postcard shows. There was a choice of seating arrangements, as well as ceiling straps for standing passengers to stabilise themselves.

The decoration of this entrance to Trafalgar Square station (now called Charing Cross) would be considered clumsy and unartistic by today's standards. In 1907 it was nevertheless eye-catching.

of London Limited, came to own most of the tube lines as well as the District Railway, three tramway companies and eventually the main bus company. Known colloquially as 'The Combine', this grouping of operators set about unifying public transport and branding all its railways under the 'Underground' banner, with free publicity maps to promote wider use of the system. In this it set in place all the key elements of London's integrated public transport operation of today.

Mrs Pennell mentioned the elevator (lift) in her description, and without lifts the tube railway would not have been possible. Passengers could hardly be expected to descend and climb stairs to and from platforms typically 60 feet below street level, so lifts were essential. Escalators were not commercially available until 1900, and so lifts were the only alternative to stairs at the original tube stations. A number of deep stations still rely on them, where installing escalators would present major problems. Examples of stations in central London that still use lifts alone include Covent Garden, Edgware Road (Bakerloo Line), Goodge Street and Russell Square. For safety reasons these lifts were installed in pairs sharing a single shaft. Each lift has an unmarked escape door facing the centre of the shaft. If one lift becomes stalled, the other lift can be lowered to the same level and the doors opened, to enable passengers to transfer to the other cage.

Some of the early tube stations failed to attract many passengers. These are the remains of City Road station in Islington. Closed in 1922, it is now used merely as a ventilation shaft.

The early tube railways were built and financed independently and it was not until 1913 that most of them were integrated into a single combine. A year before this date, the Central London still had plans to extend its line into a circular route through the West End and City.

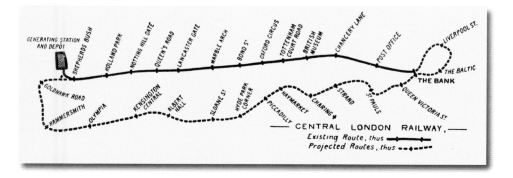

CENTRAL LONDON RAILWAY,
Existing Route, thus
Projected Routes, thus

Opening in 1906, the Piccadilly Railway was able to avoid some of the shortcomings of the first tubes. Stations were well lit, with colourful tiling and broad platforms to minimise overcrowding.

Escalators can transport people more efficiently than lifts, with less delay and irritation. One 'up' and one 'down' escalator can do the work of five lifts. The shortcomings of lifts soon became apparent and it did not take long for escalators to be installed on the Underground. The first examples were installed in 1911 at Earls Court and had the inconvenient and potentially dangerous need for passengers to 'shunt' or side-step to the right when getting off the escalator. You can see this clearly in Alfred Hitchcock's 1927 film *Downhill*. By the time this film was made, all new escalator installations were employing the improved mechanism used today, in which passengers are 'combed off' the escalator in a straight-ahead forward movement.

An example of the type of lift installed in the early twentieth century; some of these lasted eighty years in service. Note the Art Nouveau plant motifs in the iron grille above the lift gates and the wooden block indicator, which rose and fell on a rope to indicate the lift's progress.

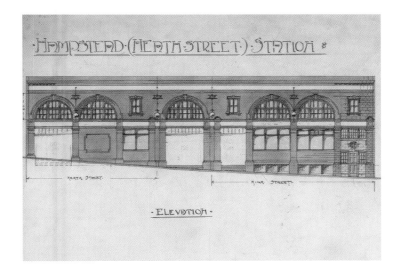

An architect's drawing of Hampstead Station. The station, still in existence, differs little from this design.

Early tube maps, such as this example of 1908, showed the lines as they would appear geographically. Not all the lines have the same colour coding as today.

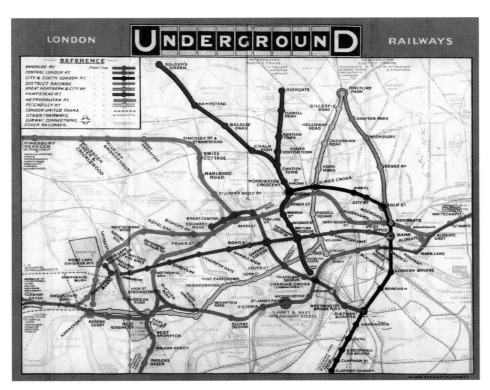

UNDERGROUND

BY
**DISTRICT
RAILWAY.**

RIGHT INTO THE HEART OF THE COUNTRY,

BOOK TO HARROW, SUDBURY OR PERIVALE.

St James' Park Station Offices, S.W.

Johnson, Riddle & Co Ltd London S.E.

UNDERGROUND TO EVERYWHERE

THE ORIGINAL Metropolitan and District railways took three decades to mature, and so, it can be argued, did the electric tube railways. By the 1920s trains were more comfortable, new stations incorporated genuinely novel architectural features, and promotional advertising had more or less come of age. The network was handling massive numbers of passengers in the peak hours, exposing the system's fundamental weakness. Under-capacity had affected the Underground almost from the outset but as London emerged from the First World War its public transport system began to struggle. Serious overcrowding on parts of the tube railway network led to optimistic plans being made for constructing new tube lines, although economic realities prevented some of these projects from coming to fruition. Nevertheless, during the mid-1920s the Underground reached further into the suburbs to develop new commuter traffic, although for the most part these new lines were built on the surface, as there was no need to tunnel in what were still mainly rural areas. In fact 55 per cent of today's Underground network runs above ground.

During the 1920s extensions reached out to Hendon Central, Edgware and Watford in the north-west and Morden in the south. In the early 1930s Stanmore was put on the tube map and the Piccadilly Line reached its northern limit at Cockfosters and its westerly target at Uxbridge. None of these localities was as urbanised or developed as today and most were either small towns and villages or else largely open fields. When the Northern Line reached Morden in Surrey in 1926 the Underground felt obliged to open a garage and filling station 'for the convenience of people who live farther afield'. The first of its kind in the country, it provided covered shelter for cycles and nearly five hundred cars, along with workshop facilities, mechanics and petrol pumps. It did not survive, even though it was expected that similar garages would be opened for season ticket holders at other outlying terminal stations.

Driving this exodus was a widely felt aspiration for better health and well-being. The middle classes in particular were urged to escape the grime

Opposite: Posters like this encouraged commuters to live further out from the city. Ironically suburbanisation soon destroyed the rural idyll.

Destination Edgware! Although an extension of the Northern Line beyond Golders Green was planned to begin in 1912, the First World War and other factors delayed construction work for a decade. The use of machinery such as this steam shovel ensured rapid progress, enabling the new line to reach Edgware by 1924.

'Pass down the platform – even loading means quicker loading and in comfort,' said this press advertisement in 1918. Human nature is slow to change and even today the message has yet to sink in.

PASS DOWN
THE PLATFORM

There are four, five, or six cars to a train. There are two gates to a car, and sometimes three. Two passengers cannot get through the same gate at the same time, but they can get through different gates at the same time. Even loading means quicker loading and in comfort.

UNDERGROUND

ELECTRIC RAILWAY HOUSE,
BROADWAY, WESTMINSTER, S.W.1

and dreariness of the inner suburbs for places with more space and light. Working in harmony, the Underground and property developers could make it possible for people to leave behind smoggy London and live instead in an electric suburb, a movement fostered by carefully planned advertising campaigns.

The pioneer of this association of interests was the Metropolitan Railway, which as far back as 1887 had formed a Surplus Lands Committee to promote housing development alongside the railway. Beginning in 1915, it issued annual booklets under the title of *Metro-Land*, giving information about locations next to its stations where readers could buy homes. It was a

Right: Embankment station (then called Charing Cross) in the 1920s, when forty-two trains passed through in each direction during the evening rush hour. Some trains ran non-stop through some stations; these fast trains had indicators beside each set of doors showing the stations not served.

Left: Where the Underground emerges overground: Hendon Central station soon after opening in 1923. Even though the station itself has barely changed since then, the open fields soon disappeared under housing – between 1921 and 1931 Hendon's population rose from 20,246 to 57,603.

A two-car off-peak train crosses the viaduct at Pymmes Brook on its way to the newly opened terminus at Cockfosters. This calendar view of 1933 was painted by Freda Lingstrom, then a poster artist and later the head of children's programmes for BBC television in the 1950s.

25

New ways were found to promote the Underground in poster art. This image promotes what we now call the 'feelgood factor'.

An eminently sensible notion was put forward in this Underground group poster of 1915.

WHY BOTHER ABOUT THE GERMANS INVADING THE COUNTRY?

INVADE IT YOURSELF BY UNDERGROUND AND MOTOR-BUS

EASTER · 1915

combination of tourist guide, amenity list and property advertiser. Publication continued annually until 1932, after which the Metropolitan was absorbed into London Transport. Guides included maps, colour photographs of beauty spots, and plentiful advertisements for house builders and furniture suppliers. The company coined the phrase 'Live in Metro-Land' and even had these words engraved on the door handles of Metropolitan Line carriages that served the stations in Metro-Land.

Encouraged by sales of this booklet, the company founded a subsidiary, Metropolitan Railway Country Estates Ltd, in 1919 to exploit the post-war demand for 'homes for heroes' and others. Noting a particular 'dearth of middle-class residences, especially in the outer suburbs of London', over the next thirteen years the company developed new residential estates following the route of the Metropolitan Line at Neasden, Wembley Park, Northwick Park, Eastcote,

Rayners Lane, Ruislip, Hillingdon, Pinner, Rickmansworth and Amersham. The company itself looked after estate planning and layout, leaving it to property developers to build the actual houses.

The other Underground lines did not actively promote new housing by advertising but stimulated interest by erecting giant information signs at the sites of new stations before construction contractors had even broken ground there. In any case, the housing developers needed little encouragement to extend what author Alan A. Jackson called *Semi-detached London*. His book of that

ELECTRIC RAILWAY TRACKS AT WEMBLEY PARK— ESTATE ON RIGHT

WEMBLEY PARK
THE IDEAL SUBURB.

name mentions a Mr Frank Howkins, who asserted in 1926 that the opening of stations with a reasonable service of trains will cause an almost sudden jump in values of adjoining land – the magic half-mile circle. He also quotes officers of the London County Council who said 'Run the trains and they [the houses] will come'. And come they did, although the new commuters did not always travel at times to suit the train operators. In 1938 London Transport noted with regret that canny white-collar workers from areas such as Morden and Edgware were taking subsidised workmen's tickets (intended for artisans, mechanics and labourers, and available only before 8 a.m.). They were overcrowding the workmen's trains and then waited about in central London stations and streets until just before 9 a.m., when their offices opened.

Outside the peak hours, relatively few people used the trains in these outer areas and in some cases, as on the Piccadilly Line to Cockfosters, shorter trains of just two coaches were run. After a while, the bother of coupling and uncoupling trains throughout the day was considered not worth the amount of electricity saved and this practice was abandoned in the 1950s. But how to attract more people to travel in the off-peak? Retail therapy was one idea and poster campaigns promoted the attraction of shopping between 10 a.m. and 4 p.m. Outdoor leisure pursuits were encouraged by cheap off-peak and weekend tickets, supported by booklets providing descriptions and maps of country rambles. The old poster catchphrase 'Underground to Everywhere' of 1908 was revived in the late 1920s, with slogans such as

Nowadays a picture of railway tracks would not be the best way to encourage people to move to Wembley, but in 1915 a reliable electric train service right next to a new estate was a powerful attraction.

Below: The delights of Metro-Land were idealised even on carriage door handles.

A poster advertising houses for sale and train services to the leafy suburbs of Metro-Land. Areas promoted included Pinner, Kenton, Kingsbury, Watford and Amersham.

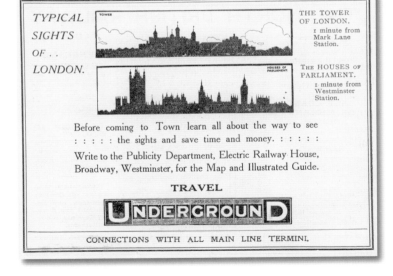

Even in simple black and white, this imaginative press advertisement made a distinctive impact. The offer of free maps and guides demonstrates the importance that the Underground put on marketing as far back as 1914.

'Underground, alight here for Everywhere' and 'The Country by Underground'. Countless other poster campaigns, backed up with free Country Walks folders, followed in succeeding decades.

Over several decades, the Underground issued numerous subsidised booklets extolling the delights of London's countryside for commuting and exploring.

But what happened to Metro-Land? Virtually forgotten after the Metropolitan lost its independent existence, its memory was revived in the 1960s by the writer and Poet Laureate Sir John Betjeman, described by *The Times* in 2007 as the 'hymnologist of Metroland'. Betjeman's personal affection for this lost land was strong. In 1960, he wrote in his autobiography: 'Metroland beckoned us out to lanes in beechy Bucks.' Thirteen years later his wistful message attained a mass audience when his documentary on this theme was broadcast on BBC television. A classic of informative broadcasting, this programme is now available on DVD to enjoy again. Whether the old spirit of Metro-Land and what it stood for have any validity today is difficult to decide, although nostalgia is certainly not what it used to be.

The Underground's promotional activities were underpinned by a wider scheme of 'arts of the Underground', including the Underground's

As the Underground matured, so did its architectural aspirations. This glass dome or cupola over Clapham Common station adds a taste of the exotic to a workaday structure, as well as making the station stand out in an unremarkable townscape.

Elements such as this attractive tile from Belsize Park station did not form part of an overall co-ordinated approach to architectural design on the Underground. After his appointment as Commercial Manager in 1912, Frank Pick made it his business to apply a more unified visual identity.

distinctive architecture, the iconic 'roundel' symbol and clear typography. The credit for all this is due to Frank Pick (1878–1941), who joined the Underground in 1907, rising to Chief Executive of London Transport in 1940. He was both a pioneer of good design and a patron of the public arts. Under Pick's influence the Underground, with its allied operations, was the first transport undertaking in Britain to apply 'best practice' design and marketing techniques across all aspects of its activity. The Underground and London Transport became one of the first organisations in Britain to develop an all-embracing corporate identity and a consistent

Decoration inside stations went beyond the mundane, with some works of genuine artistic merit, such as this mosaic fortunately retained at Maida Vale.

Design in harmony. This combined bench, windscreen and nameplate at Turnham Green sits comfortably with the notched wooden canopy valance above. London Underground takes an enlightened attitude to protecting features like these that have survived modernisation.

Given a remit of putting clarity above everything else, calligrapher Edward Johnston came up with the much imitated Johnston Sans alphabet. To many observers it looks as fresh today as it did when first introduced on tube stations in 1916.

ABCDEFGHIJKLMNOP QRSTUVWXYZ abcdefghijklmnopqrst uvwxyz 1234567890 &£

An alternative to Johnston's block letter form was commissioned from noted lettering artist Percy Delf Smith in the late 1920s. A monumental design using serifs, it was considered too formal for use on stations and only a few of the signs survive.

brand image across all its operations which was recognised by London's public at large. Pick achieved this by careful control and harmonisation of every element of design.

Before the 1920s the station architecture of the Underground had been either excessively formal or rather nondescript. Indeed, many of the earliest stations were designed by engineers, rather than architects, and made little pretence at style. The first attempt to apply a standard design was seen in the glazed-brick buildings by Leslie W. Green featuring three generously proportioned arches above the ground floor, and Art Nouveau motifs in their minor detailing (most of these stations survive). It was not until Pick commissioned the architect Charles Holden in 1925 that station styling looked to the future and followed modern styles. Pick sought a fresh look in typography as well. The Victorian letter forms in use when he joined the Underground were not applied consistently, nor were they especially easy to read. Far better would be a single style of lettering that was more balanced, more harmonious and more logical. The result was Johnston Sans, a letter face that was equally suitable for station names, route diagrams, direction indicators and posters. Launched in 1916, it is still in use today in digital form with minimal alteration (it was also the inspiration for the well-known printing typeface Gill Sans).

The Underground's emblematic roundel symbol (it has been called a 'logo for London' although it is not a logo as such) also bears the stamp of

STATION CAR PARK
FOR RAILWAY PASSENGERS CARS ONLY OPEN DAILY · TICKETS TO BE OBTAINED IN ADVANCE FROM BOOKING OFFICE. FEE 6ᴅ

Frank Pick. Dating from 1908, when it was a blue horizontal bar superimposed on a red solid circle or bullseye, it was given a makeover at Pick's request. He had seen the bar and inverted triangle symbol of the YMCA and asked for something of that quality, but more balanced. Edward Johnston, who designed the Underground's alphabet, refined the bullseye into the subtler, less cumbersome roundel. It was first employed for publicity purposes in 1919 and remains in use today.

Station architecture has for many decades been one of the 'arts of the Underground', as Park Royal exemplifies. Designed by Welch and Lander in a style known as Streamline Moderne, its buildings form very effectively a series of simple interconnecting shapes.

Fly
the Tube

Take the Piccadilly Line to Heathrow Airport.
It's the only way to fly.

platform
art

From Here
to Here

Stories inspired by the Circle line

A unique poster at every Circle line station
8 September – 10 October 2005

Platform for Art brings together London Underground staff, design students from London College of Communication, University of the Arts London, Cyan Books and the writers group 26 as part of the London Design Festival. The full stories behind these images are presented in an exhibition at London College of Communication and in a book published by Cyan.

Platform for Art is the public art programme for London Underground.
See websites for more details: www.tfl.gov.uk/pfa and www.fromheretohere.com

This project is dedicated to London.

26   A&B   CYAN

MAYOR OF LONDON   Transport for London UNDERGROUND

Above: The Underground's poster designs have
not lost their ingenuity. (The Piccadilly Line was
extended to Heathrow in 1977.)

Right: This station sign at Ealing Broadway,
probably a century old, illustrates the origin of
the Underground roundel. The solid red circle
design was introduced in 1908 and replaced by
an open ring in 1917.

Opposite:
The simplicity of today's Underground roundel
and the legibility of Johnston's clear alphabet
create a powerful branding and functional
corporate identity scheme.

Frank Pick also applied his own progressive ideas to advertising and marketing. Poster advertising was already an established art at the time he joined the Underground but over the decades Pick's patronage of leading artists such as Edward McKnight Kauffer, Jacob Epstein, Man Ray and the cartoonist Fougasse ensured that London Transport attained (and retained) a world-class reputation for its publicity posters.

Modern Wonder

TWOPENC
EVERY WEDNESDA
Vol. 3. No. 66.   Week ending August 20,

LONDON'S STREAMLINED TUBE TRAIN

here are four of these trains made up of
 cars each and developing 1,656 h.p., running
 600 volts D.C. They have greater accel-
ation and braking power and are now in
rvice on the Piccadilly Line.

great feature is that all the control gear

1. Section through London clay
2. Concrete lining   3. Section of steel tunnel
4. Asbestos-lined tunnel to eliminate noise
5, 5A. Electric windscreen wipers
6. Driver's loud-speaker
7. Tunnel lighting unit for workmen
9. Tunnel lighting cable. 9. Telephone cables

15. Automatic air brake handle
16. Joy-stick control   17. Automatic coupling
18, 18A. Live rails   19. Insulator
20. Concrete foundation for track
21. Face-plate controller
22, 22A. Contact shoes   23. Air reservoir
24. Power bogie   25. Brake cylinder and shoe

BRAVE NEW WORLD

D ESPITE the economic depression and fears of approaching war, the 1930s were marked by considerable faith in the future and an obsession with modernism. In a period sometimes dubbed the 'Machine Age', everything was new and exciting (or so it seemed). While not many could afford transatlantic air travel or the new refrigerators and television sets, nobody could fail to notice the new 'Moderne' style of architecture and the Art Deco styling being applied to just about everything else. For the Underground this was also a crucial period since public transport in London as a unified whole in terms of design and purpose originated in that 1933–9 period.

The fundamental change came in 1933, when the Underground's two private owners, Underground Electric Railways Limited and the independent Metropolitan Railway, were amalgamated, along with all buses, coaches and trams in the London area, to form a new unified public transport operator, the London Passenger Transport Board. This unsubsidised public corporation, known as 'London Transport' for short, took over on 1 July 1933. Apart from this renaming – and a new streamlined symbol that did not last long – it was business as usual for the largely unchanged operation.

When the new body began to assess its responsibilities, however, consideration was given to building faster trains and new tube lines that would modernise and improve public transport in London under a scheme known as the '1935–40 New Works Programme'. A major investment programme was developed to extend and renew the Underground, one of the first products of this being four experimental trains tested in 1936–7 and put into service on the Piccadilly Line. Influenced no doubt by the streamlining applied to motor vehicles and to trains on the main-line railways, three of the new trains were streamlined, attracting considerable attention. The rounded surfaces reduced wind resistance, particularly in tube tunnels, and were described in some press reports as improving acceleration greatly. The streamlining led to maintenance difficulties, however, and was not judged a success. A significant improvement was the enhanced acceleration, achieved by having half the axles motorised and asymmetrical

Opposite:
The 1930s obsession with speed touched London Transport, with streamlining applied to new designs of trains. Although eye-catching, the innovation turned out to offer no practical benefits and the appearance of the new trains that followed was less dramatic.

The obsession with streamlining is evident in this new trademark introduced when London's public transport providers were amalgamated into a single organisation in 1933. Uninspired and unloved, it was soon abandoned in favour of the traditional roundel.

The 1930s saw many innovations on the Underground. Although plans for streamlined trains and express tube lines bypassing less important stations failed to materialise, London acquired a network much extended into the suburbs, and many impressive new stations.

bogies that put more weight on the driven wheels. Other new trains introduced in 1937 (Metropolitan Line) and 1938 (tube lines) were given more conventional styling and lasted many years in service (some of the 1938 series are still giving good service on the Isle of Wight).

Faster trains alone would not solve overcrowding problems and consideration was also given to building brand-new 'bypass' lines that would enable trains from the outer suburbs to reach central London more quickly. This radical solution was given serious attention following an internal report of 1935 that recommended constructing new tunnels for relief lines, specifically on the Northern Line (which still suffers chronic overcrowding today). The report explained:

> A relief line, if built, might form an express line parallel to the existing line from Camden Town to Charing Cross or Waterloo or beyond, omitting three or four stations. [Another] new line would become a fast line between Kennington and Clapham Common or Balham so that Morden Line trains may use the fast line.

After a study visit to the New York subway system, the following year a team of senior staff recommended building additional express relief lines, on the Central Line between Marble Arch and Liverpool Street, on the Northern

A Piccadilly Line train at Hammersmith *c.*1935 in the bright red and cream livery then used for tube trains. Space that could have provided more seats was wasted in these trains by the motor equipment at the front of the train. This shortcoming was rectified in the next generation of trains.

Line between Highgate Archway and Tottenham Court Road, and a brand-new route from Baker Street to Victoria to relieve the Bakerloo Line. In the event none of these grandiose schemes for high-speed relief lines came to fruition although some first steps were taken in 1940 at the height of war, as described in the next chapter.

A third element of the New Works Programme consisted of plans to extend some existing lines, partly over lines belonging to the main-line railway companies. In addition steam trains would be eliminated on the outer sections of the Metropolitan Line north of Rickmansworth. This represented a significant undertaking that could not be achieved overnight, and the

The lack of streamlined ends did not take away the attraction of these sleek new trains introduced in 1937. Not obvious to passengers was their novel 'Metadyne' equipment, which improved the efficiency of the electric motors.

New tube trains built in the late 1930s had all motor equipment relocated underneath the train. The stylish varnished wood interior, the moquette seating fabric with its 'roundel' design and the green paint combine to give a warm appearance.

Innovations on the tube network were considered significant enough to interest readers of popular magazines in the 1930s. This cover illustration of 1935 showcases Osterley station, 55 Broadway, banks of escalators and signalling techniques.

outbreak of war in September 1939 meant that the vast bulk of these schemes had to be deferred until after the war (as we shall see later).

One aspect of inter-war construction that was accomplished with signal success was the provision of eye-catching new stations, along with the modernisation of existing ones. Although a number of designers and architects were employed, the man who most determined the 'new look' of the Underground was the already established architect Charles Holden. His work on stations began in 1925, when he prepared designs for the new extension to Morden. His next commission was for the Underground's headquarters offices at St James's Park (1929), which has been described as the most significant commercial building of the decade in London. Holden produced more of his admired designs for the next twenty years while managing to avoid sameness, with stations along the Piccadilly Line to Uxbridge and Cockfosters, the District Line to Hounslow and the post-war Central Line eastward extension. As well as new stations, the Underground set in motion during this period major below-street rebuilding of tube

Gaming machines on the Underground? Despite its appearance, this is actually an experimental device of the 1930s to help passengers find the most direct route to their destination.

An imaginative promotional move was the use of floodlighting to make stations more conspicuous and inviting. This is Warren Street station in 1934, illuminated by 'Osira' sodium floodlights.

stations in central London such as Leicester Square, Piccadilly Circus, Chancery Lane and St Paul's.

The same careful attention to design that characterised the architecture of the buildings was applied to minor details such as platform benches, lighting columns, signage, litter bins and even the sycamore panelling that surrounded suites of ticket machines called 'auto booking offices'. The Machine Age obsession did not pass the Underground by. Recessed sales machines appeared in the walls of booking halls and the Underground's internal telephone network was automated with letter dialling codes similar to the WHItehall 1212 numbers of London's public telephone system. Passengers in 1933 were even offered a self-service information booth with which they could find their way by twirling a dial. To enquire how to reach any point in the city, travellers set the dial according to a printed list of instructions and the machine then informed them of the place's location, the exact fare required and the number of the platform from which the appropriate train left.

A far more enduring novelty of the 1930s is the diagrammatic tube map. All previous maps of the Underground attempted to be geographically accurate, making central stations densely packed and not as clear as they

Left: Charles Holden's Southgate station in May 1933, two months after it opened. At first sight, its circular flat roof appears to hover over a horizontal band of windows, topped by an illuminated feature resembling one of the electric coils from Frankenstein's laboratory.

might have been. It was only in 1931 that Harry Beck, an unemployed engineering draughtsman, had the inspired notion of setting out the tube map in diagrammatic form, rather like an electrical circuit diagram. Routes with curves were straightened out and distance between stations adjusted to give sufficient separation on the diagram. Although his design was not well received initially, it was adopted two years later and became both an instant success and an enduring design icon, the inspiration for countless other maps and imitated worldwide. Diagrammatic route maps had appeared some time previously, above the seats in railway carriages, but Beck was the first to redesign the map of a complete network along diagrammatic lines.

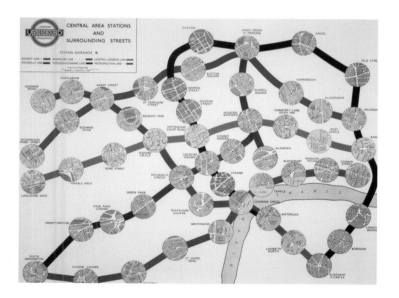

Left: In 1935 the Underground abandoned the new diagrammatic style for this experimental tube map.

43

THE UNDERGROUND AT WAR

L ONDON TRANSPORT CARRIED ON was how the story of the Underground (and London's buses) during the Second World War, published two years after the end of the hostilities, was titled. It is an apt summary but barely hints at the full extent of triumphs and tragedies, success and suffering, and much more. From the outset the Underground was under pressure, in ways that it had never experienced before: staff were directed into the fighting services, and vast resources were put into evacuating children to the provinces. Much effort was put into black-out preparations, reducing light levels on board trains and stations, fixing anti-blast netting onto windows and other necessary aggravations. Passengers encountered reduced train services that were liable to curtailment or cancellation without warning.

Behind the scenes special suites of emergency control offices for 350 key officials were set up in disused passages and platforms at Down Street, Dover Street, Hyde Park Corner, Knightsbridge and Holborn, with sleeping and feeding accommodation at some of these locations. Part of the disused station at Brompton Road was used as London's anti-aircraft gun operations control. Plotting staff here received details of enemy raids by telephone from Observer Corps centres, which in turn passed on reports from posts dotted about the country. Movements of the raiders were plotted on the map table so that commanders in the gallery could see at a glance the numbers of the enemy aircraft and the routes being taken. On this basis instructions would be sent out to the anti-aircraft gun sites that surrounded London in an attempt to intercept the enemy before they could reach the capital.

The former lift shafts of St Paul's station became the nerve centre of the nation's electricity system, allowing power resources across the country to be pooled and transferred quickly from one area to another. The lower levels of the closed Down Street station were converted into protected headquarters for the Railway Executive Committee, complete with offices, meeting rooms and a typing pool. From this location senior railway officers made arrangements for moving men, guns and ammunition by rail from one part of the country to another. The Prime Minister, Winston Churchill, and

Opposite:
Clearing up begins at Sloane Square on 13 November 1940 after a bomb reduced the station to rubble and killed seventy-nine people. While rescue workers inspect the damage, other men load rubble into goods wagons.

The 'Blitz' bombing of London that started in September 1940 led to the opening of tube stations to people sheltering from aerial attack. The thousands who took advantage of this protection caused organisational problems that London Transport sought to mitigate with this poster.

NOTICE

SHELTER
IN UNDERGROUND STATIONS

London Transport asks those who seek shelter in Underground stations to help in maintaining the essential transport facilities which are used by roundly one million passengers daily.

Passengers must be afforded free and uninterrupted use of the platforms and stations and the space used for shelter must therefore be limited. Only the space within the white lines may be used for this purpose. The police have been instructed to enforce this arrangement and those seeking shelter are asked to help them in carrying it out.

Stations and platforms must be vacated in the early morning and before the heavy passenger traffic begins.

Only a limited amount of personal baggage, etc., will be allowed on the premises.

Stations and platforms must be kept free from litter which should be carried away or placed in receptacles provided for that purpose.

LONDON ⊖ TRANSPORT

his ministers also made use of these premises for War Cabinet meetings on occasions.

Activities such as these were at least productive but the Underground's engineering staff also had to contend with major destruction by enemy bombs, the deepest of which penetrated 47 feet through solid ground. Tunnels were breached, viaducts were smashed, electric current cut off, signalling put out of action, and rolling stock either derailed or destroyed. After Granville Tunnel, between King's Cross and Farringdon, was bombed, it took nine months of hard work to restore the train service, while on the East London Line trains were suspended for months at a time. A connection off the West London Line was bombed so badly that services never resumed. One of the

To minimise the risk of bomb penetration, many tube stations acquired covered blast walls. This is Piccadilly Circus in 1944, where the 'pyramid' in the background is protecting the 'Eros' statute against damage.

Deep tube stations did not escape damage either. At Balham, on 16 October 1940, a bomb penetrated the tunnel and killed 111 people. The northbound platform seen here was filled almost to the roof with rubble. The stopped clock marks the moment when the bomb struck.

worst incidents took place in November 1940, when the newly rebuilt station at Sloane Square received a direct hit. As well as destroying most of the station, the bomb also sent a huge lump of concrete through a coach of a departing train, killing seventy-nine people.

Refreshments are served to shelterers in the medical centre at Notting Hill Gate station in December 1940. As well as light meals, London Transport provided first-aid posts with a trained nurse, and sometimes a doctor, in every station where people sheltered.

'Passed by the censor' is part of the caption for this photograph of the destroyed station at Moorgate. All sensitive pictures were examined by the Ministry of Information, which could block or delay the publication of any image that might demoralise citizens or aid the enemy.

A further complication was the public's use of tube stations as air-raid shelters. Although tube stations had never been designed as living quarters for large numbers of people and were not equipped with toilets or washing facilities at platform level, public pressure led to their use as shelters, with permits issued to individuals. At the height of the bombing raids some eighty tube stations housed thousands of families in London, grateful for the protection they afforded, even though a direct hit could – and did – penetrate down to tube platforms.

An eye-witness account of the time recalled:

By 4 p.m. all the platforms and passage space of the underground station are staked out, chiefly with blankets folded in long strips laid against the wall – for the trains are still running and the platforms in use. A woman or child guards places for about six people. When the evening comes, the rest of the family crowd in.

A warden added:

The atmosphere is generally a friendly one. Disputes are determined by the station staff, police, or wardens, with the surrounding shelterers as an unofficial jury of comment. By eleven most of the shelterers are asleep. Maintenance gangs still carry on their work on track and cables and clear the litter which a few careless hands still throw on the track.

An attendant places a record on a loudspeaker gramophone in a passage of Holborn station used as an air-raid shelter in 1941. This was the first of five similar sets for entertaining those forced underground during air raids, gifted by the American Committee for Relief of Air Raids.

This poster of 1942 is a vivid reminder of the hazards passengers faced using the Underground when normal station lighting had to be extinguished.

There were a few problems when passengers had to clamber over shelterers but the number of late evening passengers was much reduced because of the black-out and the fact that many businesses had relocated outside the centre of London.

Although the planned bypass lines mentioned in the previous chapter were never built, tunnels that could be used for that purpose were indeed constructed from 1940 onwards. In that year the Ministry of Home Security gave instructions for eight deep-level civilian shelters with sleeping accommodation for 64,000 people to be constructed by the Underground. Largely forgotten now, these deep shelters used standard tube tunnel components and were fitted out with beds, sanitary facilities and medical centres. Not all were opened

BEFORE ALIGHTING

BLACK
WARNING
OUT

LOOK FOR PLATFORM

A bomb falling into the Thames might have penetrated tube tunnels and caused serious flooding. To counteract this risk, flood gates were installed at stations on either side of the river. These workmen are installing a gate at Charing Cross (now Embankment) station in November 1943.

to civilians, some being used for military and security purposes. The locations were Clapham South, Clapham Common, Clapham North, Stockwell, Chancery Lane, Goodge Street, Camden Town and Belsize Park. Traces of most of these can still be seen at surface level and the majority are in use now as storage facilities, the express tube lines having never been built.

This is Clapham South – not the tube station but a deep shelter for civilians built in tube-style tunnels below the Northern Line platforms. Eight of these shelters were built, each with bunk beds for eight thousand people. Today the shelter is used for secure storage.

Equally fantastic was the underground factory built between Redbridge and Gants Hill in tunnels that had been constructed for the Central Line's eastern extension. Completion of the new railway had been halted by the war and no track had been laid in these tunnels, making them suitable for conversion into 300,000 square feet of production facilities, complete with first-aid rooms and a canteen for six hundred people. In this factory a total of two thousand workers (mainly female) worked shifts around the clock producing aircraft materials that totalled 18 million shell and bomb cases, 11 million connectors for aircraft wiring, 74,000 wiring harnesses, 28,000 aircraft pumps and 23,000 engine cartridge starters.

One of the most unusual aspects of the Underground during the Second World War was the use of disused passages and stations to house the nation's treasures. Aldwych station, which was closed during the war, became the home of the British Museum's famous Elgin Marbles, while part of Piccadilly Circus station housed art treasures from the Tate Gallery and London Museum. Equally surprising was the production of torpedo sights and other war equipment in a part of Earls Court station.

In twin tunnels almost 2½ miles long, built (but not yet completed) for an extension of the Central Line, a factory was created for producing war materials. Normally the narrow-gauge train delivered and collected materials but in this view of October 1942 aircraft industry executives from the United States are using it to make an inspection tour.

THE ELIZABETHAN ERA

W HEN THE Second World War ended in 1945 the Underground system was in a run-down state, with a significant proportion of its stations and rolling stock damaged or destroyed. None of its optimistic New Works targets for extending the Central and Northern lines had come to fruition, even though these plans had been so advanced that telephone numbers for the new stations had appeared in the 1940 edition of London Transport's internal telephone directory. Despite this, ambitious plans were laid for new rolling stock and rebuilding stations. By 1948 most of the Central Line extensions were completed, although the Epping–Ongar section remained steam-operated until 1957. The westerly extension beyond West Ruislip to Denham was abandoned, along with the Northern Heights extensions of the Northern Line to Bushey Heath, when post-war legislation restricted development of land in the 'green belt' surrounding outer London. Because of the shortage of funds in this era of austerity, the tunnels constructed during the war as deep-level air-raid shelters were not to be linked up for constructing new high-speed tube railways, and the Bakerloo Line extension to Camberwell Green and the Northern Line branch to Alexandra Palace, which were shown on tube maps for a couple of years, were abandoned.

The first major investment in constructing new lines came in the 1960s. In 1961 electrification of the Metropolitan Line was extended from Rickmansworth to Amersham and Chesham, with the northward section to Aylesbury handed over to British Rail. Seven years later the Victoria Line was opened, London's first entirely new tube line in decades. It heralded several innovations: it was the first instance of an entire line using automatic train control based on an electronic safety signalling and driving command system. The train operator's duties were and are confined to opening and closing the train doors and pressing the 'start' button, leaving acceleration, braking and stopping to the automatic equipment. Every station was equipped with automatic fare collection equipment, and all but one of the line's stations provided interchange with another line.

Opposite:
On 16 December 1977 the tube reached Heathrow Airport, with the Queen riding in the cab of the first train on this auspicious occasion.

The post-war aspirations for completing the pre-war New Works Programme are illustrated in this graphic. The extensions to West Ruislip in the west and Epping and Ongar in the east were carried out but the new routes to Bushey Heath and Alexandra Palace were abandoned.

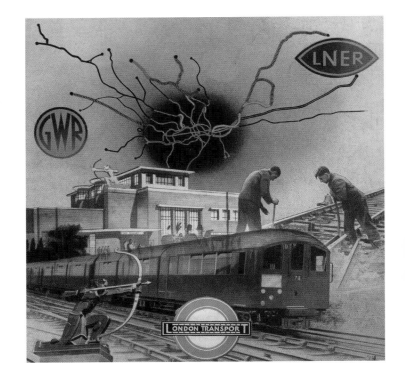

Part of the ill-fated 'Northern Heights' extension scheme, these unused platforms lost in the undergrowth at Highgate were built for Northern Line trains from Moorgate to Alexandra Palace that never materialised.

The Victoria Line has been a remarkable success. Although it was designed to shorten journey times in central London and relieve overcrowding in other lines of the Underground, it generated significant new passenger traffic and demonstrated the need for additional tube lines. The result was the Jubilee Line from Stanmore to Stratford via the Dockland regeneration zone (opened in 1979 and extended in 1999). Planned as the 'Fleet Line', this addition to the Underground took over a section of the Bakerloo Line between Stanmore and Baker Street and extended it through central London to a temporary terminus at Charing Cross, from where it was intended to cross the City of London to reach New Cross and New Cross Gate. Changing priorities and massive urban renewal in the Docklands area caused a change of plan to bring the line alongside the Thames to Docklands and Stratford. In technical terms, the Jubilee Line extension of 1999 is the most advanced section of the Underground, with dramatic modern station architecture, step-free access from street levels to the platforms and

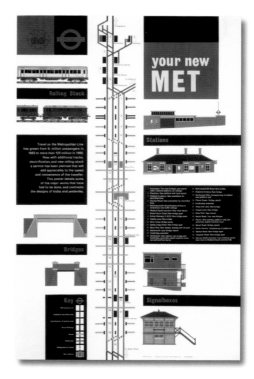

glass protection barriers on the roomy platforms to prevent people from falling on the track. Gates in these barriers open automatically and provide access to

Numerous new-build and reconstruction projects characterised the post-war era. This poster from 1960 by William Fenton celebrates the 'new for old' replacement activities on the Metropolitan Line to Amersham.

A significant modernisation milestone was reached when the Metropolitan Line was electrified to Amersham in 1961 with trains that are still running today.

The Victoria Line, opened in 1968, followed a brand-new route that relieved pressure on other lines of the Underground. Tiled motifs differentiated each station visually.

Passengers found the new Victoria Line trains agreeably roomy but their real novelty was automatic control; the train operator (driver) is required only to close the train doors and press a pair of buttons to start the train.

trains only when these have stopped so that their doors align exactly with the openings in the barrier. The line's signalling system is being upgraded to support automatic train operation in the future.

The Docklands Light Railway (DLR) is another new construction and forms a complex mesh of east–west and north–south lines on the east and south-east sides of London opened in stages between 1987 and 2009, and still not complete. Although shown on tube maps, and part of Transport for London, the DLR is not part of the Underground. Fully automatic in operation (trains have no driver), the system is considered a 'light metro' and is built more simply (and economically) than a normal railway, using trains that are no more substantial than urban trams.

In the background of this photograph of Canada Water station is the glass barrier that prevents passengers from falling onto the track. The doors open only when a train is aligned exactly behind them.

Although shown on tube maps, the Docklands Light Railway is not operated by London Underground. Described as a 'light metro' system, it is a cross between a train and a tram. This is West India Quay station.

What is historically London Underground's newest tube line is the short Waterloo & City Line, which was not a new construction but joined the system only in 1994. It had opened as long ago as 1898 but for nearly a hundred years it was always operated by the railway company responsible for Waterloo main-line terminus (latterly British Rail). When the national railway system was privatised it appeared inappropriate for one London tube line to have a different status from the rest of the system. By agreement, ownership of 'the Drain' (as this line is often known) was transferred to London Underground, and between April and September 2006 the trains, tunnels, platforms, depot, track and signalling underwent major refurbishment.

Many stations have seen refurbishment in recent years. At Baker Street the Bakerloo Line platforms have had new tiling that features a silhouette of the fictional detective Sherlock Holmes, who famously lived at 221B Baker Street.

A welcome improvement to passenger information is the electronic 'next train' indicator, introduced from 1983. This model on trial at St James's Park station in 1981 replaces the device in the distance behind.

The London Transport Museum at Covent Garden was refurbished between 2005 and 2007. There is a back-up museum store that the public can visit on open days. Part of the museum's collection of station signs is seen here.

As well as expansion and technical innovation, the period since the Second World War also saw major organisational change. As part of London Transport, the Underground began this period within a public corporation with an independent public service remit. From this the operation progressed, if that is the word, by stages into a far more politically driven body. Nationalised in 1948 as the London Transport Executive (LTE), the Underground now came within the aegis of central government and its ideological agendas. The short title 'London Transport' remained in use, as it continued to do when the LTE was reformed in 1963 as the London Transport Board. Further change came in 1985, when London Transport's bus and Underground operations were separated from the overall management of transport in London. The Underground system became the standalone business London Underground Limited (LUL) and since 2003 has been a wholly owned subsidiary of Transport for London (TfL). TfL is a statutory corporation regulated under local government finance rules. The Mayor of London has direct influence over the running of TfL, determining the structure and level of public transport fares in London and appointing the board members.

With greater politicisation has come stronger marketing and direction towards what might be called people-pleasing activities. One fruit of these has been the rebirth of the London Transport Museum, which had previously languished. In 1980 the museum relocated from Syon Park in west London to a convenient central location in one of the old Victorian market halls of Covent Garden. Between 2005 and 2007 the museum was transformed in a

£22 million refurbishment scheme to house a much expanded display showcasing the history of all forms of public transport in the London area. Enhanced shop, refreshment and educational facilities were also provided in what is now one of London's most popular visitor attractions.

Supporting the museum are a back-up store and administrative centre at Acton, west London, known as the Museum Depot. As well as being a store for historical documents and images, it is also the base for the museum's curatorial and conservation staff. The majority of the Museum's artefacts that are not on display in the main museum are kept here, together with items too large to display at Covent Garden.

This giant crane was the most effective way to remove these carriages from the Waterloo & City Line when it was closed for six months during 2006 for refurbishment.

FURTHER READING

Bayman, R. *Underground Official Handbook*. Capital Transport Publishing, 2008.

Beard, A., and Emmerson, A. *London's Secret Tubes*. Capital Transport Publishing, 2007.

Blake, J., and James, J. *Northern Wastes: Scandal of the Uncompleted Northern Line*. North London Transport Society, 1993.

Bownes, B., and Green, O. *London Transport Posters*. Lund Humphries, 2008.

Connor, J. *London's Disused Underground Stations*. Capital Transport Publishing, 2001.

Day, J., and Reed, J. *The Story of London's Underground*. Capital Transport Publishing, 2008.

Demuth, T. *Spread of London Underground*. Capital Transport Publishing, 2004.

Emmerson, A. *The Underground Pioneers*. Capital Transport Publishing, 2000.

Glover, J. *London's Underground*. Ian Allan, 2003.

Glover, J. *London's Underground Stations in Colour*. Ian Allan, 2009.

Green, O. *Underground Art: London Transport Posters 1908 to the Present*. Cassell, 1991.

Halliday, S. *Amazing and Extraordinary London Underground Facts*. David & Charles, 2009.

Harris, C. *What's in a Name? Origins of Station Names on the London Underground*. Capital Transport Publishing, 2001.

Howes, J. *Johnston's Underground Type*. Capital Transport Publishing, 2000. (Typography.)

Jackson, A. J. *London's Metroland*. Capital Transport Publishing, 2006.

Menear, L. *London Underground Stations*. Midas Books, 1983. (Architecture.)

Powers, A. *End of the Line? The Future of London Underground's Past*. Victorian Society and Thirties Society, 1987.

Rose, D. *The London Underground, A Diagrammatic History*. Capital Transport Publishing, 2007.

Taylor, S., and Green, O. *The Moving Metropolis: A History of London's Transport*. Laurence King, 2001.

Wolmar, C. *The Subterranean Railway*. Atlantic Books, 2005.

PLACES TO VISIT

ARCHITECTURAL GEMS

Picking the best of these is not easy but the following locations are worth a visit.

Arnos Grove. The 1932 station here shares the honours with Southgate as the pinnacle of Charles Holden's designs. It was named by *The Guardian* as the 'king, queen and all princes of a metro station'.

Canary Wharf. Both the steel and glass entrance arch and the interior of this 1999 station (by Norman Foster) are stunning.

Chiswick Park. The semicircular building by Charles Holden dates from 1932.

East Finchley. The prominent statue of an archer on top of the station (designed by Eric Aumonier) was unveiled in 1940.

Loughton. Continental-looking station built in 1940 to the design of John Murray Easton.

Maida Vale. Attractive large mosaics date from the station's opening in 1915.

Newbury Park. The attached bus station of 1949 (designed by Oliver Hill) is arguably more interesting than the station itself.

Osterley. Dating from 1934, this station by Charles Holden is surmounted by a huge brick tower and concrete obelisk.

St James's Park. Offices at 55 Broadway, above the station. When completed in 1929, this was the tallest office building in London. External sculptures by Jacob Epstein and Eric Gill distinguish this monolithic structure, and parts of the ground floor are accessible to visitors.

Southgate. Another Streamline Moderne concrete masterpiece by Charles Holden (1933). This one is low-profile and completely circular, forming the focal point of a shopping centre. The nearby bus shelters are equally spectacular, as were the original direction signposts, since removed.

Southwark. The key feature of this glassy station of 1999 is its 'subterranean landscape' made unique by a concourse of blue cut-glass designed by the artist Alexander Beleschenko.

TIMEWARP LOCATIONS

The following stations are some that retain attractive nooks and crannies that have survived modernisation. All are accessible except Aldwych, which is no longer open to the public.

Hammersmith station (Hammersmith & City Line) resembles a main-line terminus in miniature. This is not surprising as, like some other stations on this line, it was built by the Great Western Railway in a joint-venture project.

Aldgate

Aldwych (exterior only accessible)

Barons Court

Chalk Farm

Edgware Road (Bakerloo Line)

Hammersmith (Hammersmith & City Line)

Maida Vale

Mansion House

Temple (a tube map of 1932 is preserved outside the station)

OTHER PLACES TO VISIT

London Transport Museum, Covent Garden Piazza, London WC2E 7BB. A comprehensive museum with a vast number of exhibits, large and small (with a café and museum shop as well). Website: www.ltmuseum.co.uk/visiting/106.aspx

The Museum Depot at Acton Town. The Museum Depot is the museum's storage facility, open regularly for special events. Website: www.ltmuseum.co.uk/visiting/106.aspx

TIME TRAVEL

If you enjoy travelling in old Underground trains you can still do this. Pre-war tube trains provide the service between Ryde and Shanklin on the Isle of Wight (www.southwesttrains.co.uk/island-line.aspx), while wooden compartment coaches from the steam days of the Underground run on special vintage train days on the Bluebell Railway in Sussex (www.bluebell-railway.co.uk/) and the Kent & East Sussex Railway (www.kesr.org.uk/). You can also see old Underground trains at the Buckinghamshire Railway Centre (www.bucksrailcentre.org/). A section of the Central Line in Essex is being rebuilt as a preserved railway between Epping and Ongar (www.eorailway.co.uk/).

INDEX